The Coloring Book
Blessed Carlo Acutis

Teenage Hero of Christ's Real Presence in the Eucharist

Carlo Acutis was born in London on May 3, 1991, to Italian parents, Andrea and Antonia Acutis. He was baptized on May 18th at the Church of Our Lady of Dolours in London. When he was three months old, the family moved back to Milan, Italy.

Carlo was an only child. His mother worked full-time, so he had several nannies.
One was a devout Catholic from Poland.
She often spoke to little Carlo about God, Jesus, and the Virgin Mary.

His parents also enrolled him in religious nursery schools. Carlo began to ask his parents questions about Jesus and Mary which were often very deep for a young child. He often thought about God and prayed.

Carlo's questions often left his mother bewildered, so she enrolled in a theology class.
This class was the beginning of her own spiritual journey.

Carlo began to ask his parents to bring him to Italian monasteries and convents on the weekends. He especially loved to visit Assisi. He said, "Can you believe that St. Francis actually walked these streets? And St. Clare, too? It's like being in Heaven."

As a young boy, Carlo was filled with a desire to receive Jesus in Holy Communion. Carlo's pastor allowed him to receive his First Communion at the age of seven. From that day onward, Carlo went to Mass every day to receive Communion. Carlo's reverence for the Eucharist impressed everyone.

Carlo liked to play with his animals. He had dogs, cats, and fish.
Carlo and his cousin, Flavia, made films about the animals, and Carlo would edit them into little movies.

Carlo would make his dog, Crumb, the superhero of these movies: "Little Star, the Overweight Dog!" Whenever he could, however, Crumb would sneak into Carlo's room to steal Carlo's teddy bear to play with.

His dog, Claire, would be "The Supreme Rat," who was out to conquer all the evil cats in the world —but Little Star would always win.

Soon Carlo developed a new passion: computer programming. So, Carlo's mother bought him some university-level books on the subject. At the age of 8, Carlo was able to learn several computer programming languages all by himself.

Carlo loved playing sports. In the winter, he liked skiing in the mountains. He played soccer, tennis, basketball, and learned karate. He also loved to ride his bike around the neighborhood with other boys his age.

Carlo also had a Playstation for games, but he decided to limit his gaming time to one hour on Saturdays. "I can't waste time," he told his mother. "I feel like there is so much I need to do with my life. Every minute that passes is a minute less for us to serve God."

When Carlo was eleven, he combined his love for helping others with his faith and became a catechist for younger children. The parish priest was astounded at how well he could explain the Faith to children.

Carlo liked to tell children that Jesus is the Good Shepherd,
Who always takes care of and protects everyone in His Church.

Carlo became intensely interested in miracles of the Eucharist and wanted to tell the whole world about them. "I will build a website that will describe every Eucharistic miracle that has ever happened in the history of the world!" he decided. The website he created took four years to complete.

For Carlo, daily prayer was a heartfelt conversation in which he spoke with and listened to God. He said, "When you stand in front of the sun, you get sunburned. When you stand before Jesus in the Eucharist, you become a saint."

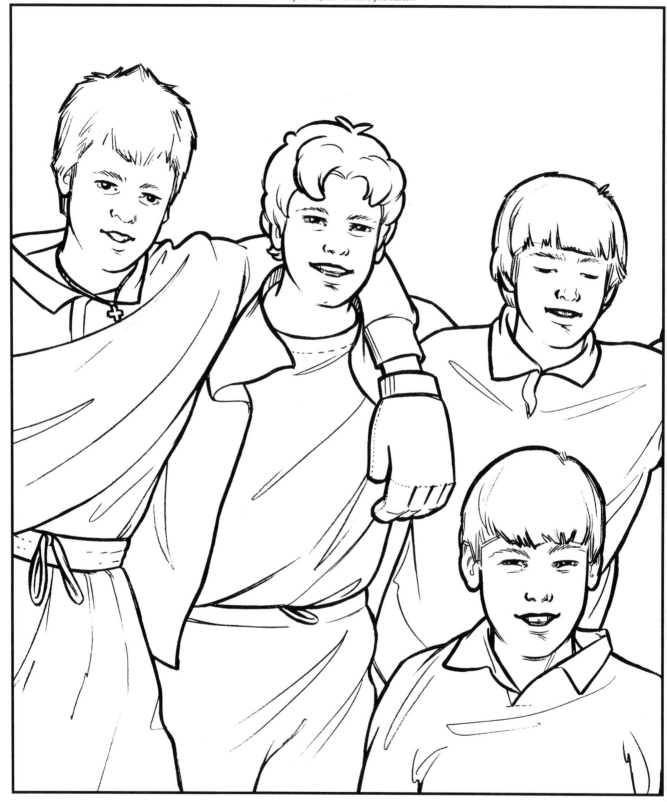

In school, Carlo was attentive to those who needed help. Whenever he noticed people being left out or bullied, he personally befriended them and brought them into his group of friends.

Carlo loved computers, but he realized that social media made people self-centered. "People are always putting their own pictures on the internet … trying to put themselves in first place, instead of God." He thought people felt too much pressure to conform. He said, "All of us are born as originals, but most of us die as photocopies."

As Jesus said: 'Truly I tell you, whatever you did for one of the least of these, you did for Me.' Carlo took this Bible passage to heart and used his allowance money to buy blankets and sleeping bags for the homeless people he met on his city's sidewalks.

In 2006, when Carlo was 15 years old, he became very ill. So, his parents brought him to a hospital in Milan. The doctors discovered that Carlo would soon die from a severe type of leukemia.

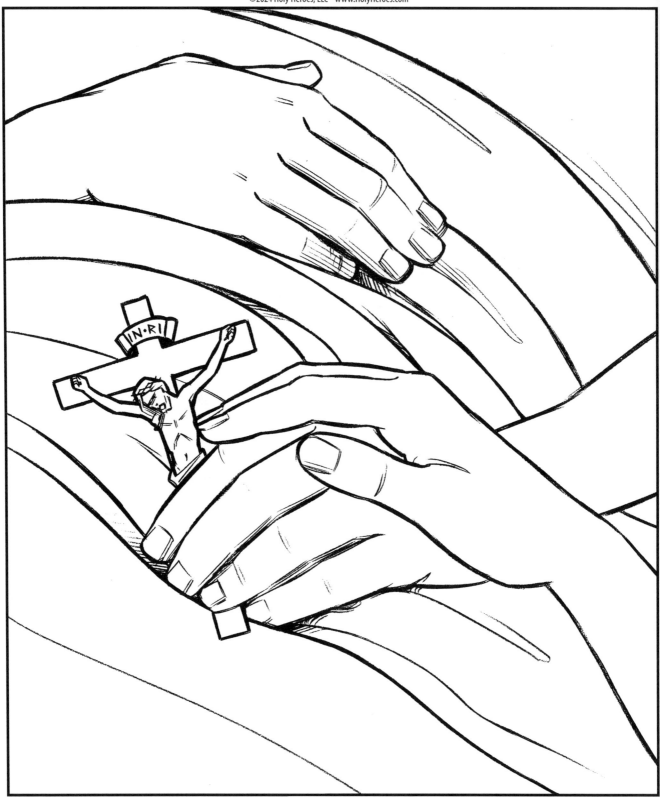

Carlo told his mother not to worry about him dying. "Mama, I will give you signs that I am with God in Heaven. I die happy, because I did not spend my life wasting time on things that are not pleasing to God."

Carlo said, "My life plan is always to be connected to Jesus. Heaven is our destination—our real homeland, where we can be with Him forever! Just think of it: The Good Shepherd has been expecting each one of us in Heaven—since before time began!"

When he was in the hospital, Carlo said, "I am offering up all my sufferings for the Pope and the Church. Offering them all up in order to go not to Purgatory—but straight to Heaven!"
Carlo died on October 12, 2006, only three days after being diagnosed with leukemia.

Four years to the day after his death, Carlo's mother gave birth to twins, a boy and a girl.
Antonia knew the twins were gifts from God to show that her son, Carlo, was now a big brother in Heaven!
In the years that followed, hundreds of miracles were reported, attributed to prayers to Carlo.

Years later, Carlo appeared to Antonia in a dream. "Mother, I will be beatified soon, and shortly after, canonized." Indeed, on October 10, 2020, only 14 years after his death, Carlo Acutis was declared, Blessed Carlo Acutis. His tomb is in his beloved Assisi, where Saint Francis is also buried.

 Carlo's "Kit" for Becoming a Saint

1. Try to go to Holy Mass and receive Holy Communion every day.
2. If you can, go to Confession every week—even if just to confess your venial sins.

 Carlo's "Kit" for Becoming a Saint
3. You have to want to be a saint with all your heart—pray to God for this grace.
4. Remember to recite the Rosary every day.

 Carlo's "Kit" for Becoming a Saint

5. Read a little bit of the Holy Bible every day.
6. Adore Jesus, truly present in the Eucharist, each day—and you will grow in holiness.

 Carlo's "Kit" for Becoming a Saint
7. Make sacrifices and self-denials frequently to Jesus and Mary to help others.
8. Ask your Guardian Angel to help you all the time—rely on him as your best friend.

Make Blessed Carlo Acutis cards for your family and friends. Color these cards, cut them out, fold them in half and give them to people you love.

BLESSED CARLO SAID:

"The more Eucharist
we receive,
the more we
become like Jesus!"

Love Jesus!

He is truly
present in the
Holy Eucharist.

_____

Tell people about Jesus in the Holy Eucharist, like Blessed Carlo did. Live in communion with Jesus, every day!

BLESSED CARLO SAID:

"The Eucharist
is my highway
to Heaven!"

Love Jesus!

He is truly
present in the
Holy Eucharist.

_____